For Evie, Abcdéé, and Créé

ISLAND HERITAGE™
175 Kahelu Avenue
Mililani, Hawai'i 96789
Orders: (800) 468-2800
Information: (808) 564-8800
Fax: (808) 564-8877
welcometotheislands.com
COP190705

ISBN: 1-61710-410-8
First Edition, First Printing—2019

The Castle That KAI Built

Written & Illustrated by

Tammy Yee

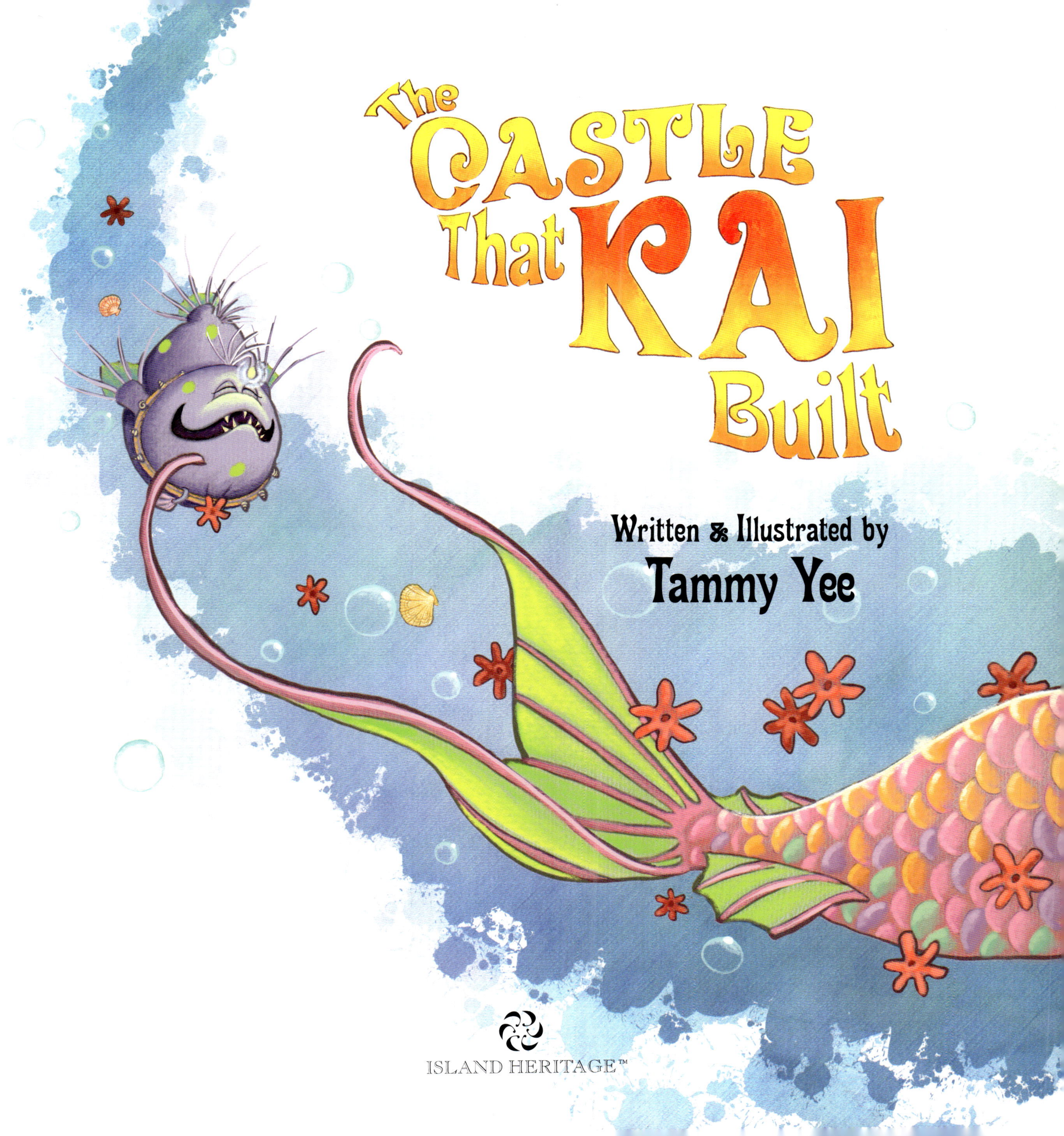

ISLAND HERITAGE™

2

Sea Piggy

This is the CLAM
that lived in the castle that Kai built.

This is the OCTOPUS
6

that tickled the clam
that lived in the castle that Kai built.

These are the JELLYFISH

that danced for the octopus
that tickled the clam
that lived in the castle that Kai built.

This is the TURTLE
10

that swooped through the jellyfish
that danced for the octopus
that tickled the clam
that lived in the castle that Kai built.

12

13

that nipped the turtle
that swooped through the jellyfish
14

that danced for the octopus
that tickled the clam
that lived in the castle that Kai built.

15

These are the
DOLPHINS

that chased the shark
that nipped the turtle
that swooped through the jellyfish
that danced for the octopus
that tickled the clam

18

19

20

21

This is the MERMAID
that cheered the dolphins
that chased the shark
that nipped the turtle
that swooped through the jellyfish
that danced for the octopus   that tickled the clam
that lived in the castle that Kai built.

22

This is the MERBOY
that kissed the mermaid
that cheered the dolphins

that chased the shark
that nipped the turtle
that swooped through the jellyfish
that danced for the octopus   that tickled the clam
that lived in the castle that Kai built.

And this is the WHALE

that sang of the merboy
that kissed the mermaid
that cheered the dolphins

28

that chased the shark
that lived in the castle that Kai built.
that tickled the clam
that nipped the turtle
that danced for the octopus
that swooped through the jellyfish

The End

Can you find Kai's friends?
Search for the colorful creatures that follow along on Kai's crazy adventure!
A
B   Clown Fish
C
D
Sea Snail
Jellyfish
Clam
F
Sea Piggy
E
G
Anglerfish
H
I
Remora
Sea Horse
Pufferfish
Answers: A) 11, B) 20, C) 3, D) 23, E) 17, F) 8, G) 14, H) 16, I) 24